AF879393

HANG ON TO IT·GIRL

THE WILY WOMAN'S GUIDE TO WILLS

First edition published in 2015

Published by Brief Books, Mooloolaba, Queensland, Australia 4557
National Library of Australia Cataloguing-in-Publication entry
Creator: Brennan, Paul, 1954- author.
Title: Hang on to it girl: the wily woman's guide to wills/ Paul Brennan.
ISBN-13: 9780987489418 (paperback)
Subjects: Wills–Australia.
Finance, Personal–Australia.
Women–Australia–Finance, Personal.
Dewey Number: 346.94054
Cartoons by Paul Brennan

Other Authors/Contributors: Edited and proofed by Kathleen Brennan

PO Box 27, Mooloolaba, Queensland, Australia 4557
BN22069914 ABN 60 583 357 067.
Phone: 07 5438 8199
info@brennanlaw.com.au
www.lawanddisorder.com.au.

For other publications by the author go to Amazon or
http://www.lawanddisorder.com.au/books.html

Book Interior design by Rue V. Cataquez (rjcc24@yahoo.com)
Front Cover design by Luke Perkins Graphics

DEDICATION

In memory of Judge John Fortgang.

My long suffering, kind Principal during my articles of clerkship.

PRAISE FOR:

HANG ON TO IT GIRL

THE WILY WOMAN'S GUIDE TO WILLS

Western Australia

"Great read, well done!"
Reg Biddulph
Biddulph & Turley

New South Wales

"I know some ladies that would enjoy this great read, but what about a man's version to keep it even?"
Susan O'Rourke
O'Rourke & Associates

"Gold."
Gary Lees
Lees Lawyers

"An enjoyable read ... there are many salient points that are true to life."
Adam Stack
Adam Stack & Co

Victoria

"It's funny because it's true..."
Jennifer Jackson, Moores

Queensland

"Great read, entertaining but to the point."
Greg Lane
Gill & Lane Solicitors
"A go-er in every waiting room."
Jeneve Frizzo,
O'Connor Law

"A very entertaining read. Love it!"
Kellie Keenan
Bennett & Philp Lawyers

"Very clever. I found the section on "Kidders" particularly poignant. Well done for adding humour to a very sober topic."
Mehera Saunders
Solicitor and Accredited Specialist

"Mercifully short."
John Fytit
Lawyer

DISCLAIMER

The content of this book is to give you legal basics and in some instances, included unashamedly to try and make you laugh. In law, it is sometimes difficult to work out what is serious and what is just for fun. The law in each jurisdiction has technical differences e.g. time limits. However, it is often very similar and therefore an international understanding is useful especially where overseas rich relative are concerned. Therefore, if you plan to do anything legal, rely on your own lawyer's advice. Not only will I deny responsibility for the legal content but also for some of the jokes.

PREFACE

I recently gave a talk to Zonta the professional women's group. When I asked who had experienced will and inheritance issues in their families, ninety percent of the group put up their hands. This may have been a particularly litigious group, but it does highlight a growing problem.

Women today are either richer and living longer or, with the wrong choice of husband, poorer and left to pick up the pieces.

Living longer gives women more time to marry even more disastrously than they did the first, second and in some cases, third time.

The security of having money can lead to pressure from those who wish you to share it. The more money, the bigger the problems.

Many of the problems are predictable. After all, it is your family.
But more importantly, many of the problems are avoidable.

PEDANTIC IDOL
律師
DESPITE THE TOUGH JUDGING THE 43 YEAR OLD PROBATE LAWYER DOMINATED THE "TEDIOUS EMAIL" CATEGORY

CONTENTS

AND I HAVE TAKEN INTO ACCOUNT YOUR PREVIOUS GOOD CHARACTER AND THAT YOU ARE MY MOTHER
BUT.....
律師
Brennan

LEGAL ADVICE ABOUT SONS TO MOTHERS

Q. I have always been very proud of my son but now he tells me that he wants to put me in a home. Must I go?

A. You are not alone. Sons, often egged on by wicked daughters-in-law, start to give hints about retirement homes at any time after their mother's 55th birthday.

Your lawyer will advise you of the five point "We Are Staying Put, Son" ("WASPS") strategy.

Use this to make your son's interjections into your life a less pleasurable experience for him until he backs off.

1. Hide all family heirlooms, rings, carpets, watches etc., to stop him visiting you just for the pleasure of inspecting them and declaring which ones will be his.

2. If you cannot bring yourself to find an outspoken lesbian lover, invent one.

3. Adopt a poison will clause. This is similar to the "poison pill" strategy that companies use to avoid takeovers. You incorporate a clause in your will which leaves your son's share of your estate to someone else. Even rich sons will baulk at the thought of their inheritance being left to say, a donkey sanctuary.

4. Stop taking hand outs from your son. Bolster your income by taking in washing, playing more bingo, seeking out senior bargains or by simply taking a rich, and preferably childless lover.

5. Avoid displays of aggressive hatred, especially those that lead to police involvement. Any sign of mental instability may enable your son to take over your affairs. Psychiatrists may be on your son's side; they have mothers themselves.

As one godmother said, "Keep your enemies close and your adult sons even closer."

MUTUAL WILLS - PROTECTING YOUR INHERITANCE

The sensible way to deal with the anguish of losing control over your money after death is to make mutual wills.

They are ordinary wills that are covered by a contract where you both agree to follow the terms of the wills even after one of you dies. The contract aspect forms a constructive trust which must be observed by your husband and his executor after you are gone.

Wives can use mutual wills to ensure that their money will eventually be inherited by their children and not some floozy. Also, wives can use it to ensure that the children of their first husband inherit their wealth rather than their step children, being the children of their second husband.

Once made, if you want to change a mutual will, you must get the agreement of your husband to rescind the contract with him, otherwise you are stuck. You could consider divorcing him, which will terminate the arrangement, but after he has died that is not an option.

TRUSTS AND ESTATES DEPT.
LOW CARBON EMISSIONS
律師
Brennan

Once your children know that the money is in the bag, they could marry even more unwisely, or give full vent to their drinking and gambling.

Due to your commitment under the mutual wills, you would be powerless to stop your money being squandered once it is inherited by your children.

Even if you squandered it yourself, you could mistime this and end up in the gutter with thoughts of suicide. Your husband will be to blame, but as he will be gone, that is hardly consolation.

Note: Although this article is directed at wives, husbands are in exactly the same position, except that Spanish waiters rather than floozies have a greater role.

NOW LET'S GET THIS RIGHT. WE PUT ALL OF OUR MONEY IN YOUR TRUST ACCOUNT AND YOU LOST IT?
律師
Brennan
CONVEYANCING LAWYER GAGS

YOU AND YOUR MONEY

Most people accept that they cannot take it with them. However, having made your money, the law will ensure that your will is carried out, provided that you lived like a monk, avoided relationships (sexual or otherwise), had no children (even in a moment of weakness) and refused to give any money away to anyone.

If you failed to do any of this, a claim could be made against your estate by a spouse, child or dependant, on the basis that you did not make adequate provision for the claimant's proper maintenance, education, and advancement in life.

* Your "children" may now include adopted children and step children. "Spouse" may include your de facto and/ or civil partner. In fact, anyone (male or female) that you have "shacked up with" for a while e.g. two years or more.

The claim is only against your "estate" which does not include property held as joint tenants (e.g. often your home), insurance policies, superannuation and trusts.

* It depends on jurisdiction

MARKETING FOR LAWYERS
TIP # 5. BE PROACTIVE
NURSING
HOME
律師
HAS ANYONE HERE GOT ANY
CHANGES TO THEIR WILL TODAY?

Unless there are good reasons for the delay, a claim must be made within a set period** of e.g. 6 or 9 months.

The court will determine if you made adequate provision for a claimant. It takes into account all the circumstances, including: the applicant's financial position, the size of your estate, the relationship that the claimant had with you (or lack of it) and the other deserving people that you have left behind.

The court will not make an order in favour of claimants who have enough money of their own. This tends to be rare, especially in the case of children. Also, the court can bar undeserving claimants.

Needy prodigal sons are in with a chance to get something; the stronger their need, the more reprehensible their conduct must be before a court will disentitle them altogether.

Costs are usually awarded out of the estate but not always.** However, claimants who have persisted in an unreasonable claim, especially where the estate is quite small, can be ordered to pay costs.

The good news is that they must all wait until you are dead and there is no need to rush.

** It depends on jurisdiction

THE MARRIAGE WAS OVER

KIDDERS-THE LATEST THREAT TO YOUR HAPPY RETIREMENT

With the savings of many parents effectively halved due to the financial crisis and their home values under siege, few are ready for the next tidal wave- KIDDERS, "Kids in debt, diligently eroding retirement savings."

In the good times, parents encouraged their children to buy homes, investment units, enter business deals, invest in shares and generally "do it" in order to get them off their hands.

Now as these financial arrangements unravel, kids need money to stave off banks or other financiers. Kids who find that they can't walk away from their problems are turning to their parents to "fix it".

READ IT CAREFULLY AND IF BY PAGE 38 YOU HAVE LOST THE WILL TO LIVE... IT IS QUITE NORMAL
律師
Brennan
THE TRUST LAWYER

Here are 5 "tough love" options for parents to adopt to protect themselves and their kids:

1. Sometimes it is better to let your kids go bust and be around to pick up the pieces.
2. A threat to be sued is not the same as being sued, and sometimes suing or being sued can be a slow process. Do not be spooked into action that you may regret.
3. Document and try to secure any loan.
4. Don't panic and use your available cash and credit cards to pay your kids' debts. You may need that cash and credit for essential items as the situation gets worse.
5. Signing a guarantee may take the heat off but it is the easiest way for you to lose your savings and your home. Creditors will pursue your kids harder if they think you care and may foot the bill. Pretend that you do not care (you will find this is easier than you think).

Most parents devote their lives to solving their kids' problems e.g. car crashes (especially if it was the parents' car) or making the occasional visit to the police station to bail their kids out.

However, when asked to make the ultimate sacrifice of delivering up their entire life savings, the best advice to loving parents is, "Don't."

FORGET PROPERTY. BUY A WILL FOR A RICH UNCLE AND WAIT
律師
INVESTMENT SEMINAR

LAST ORDERS- ALCOHOLIC SONS

Your son's drinking and gambling have far exceeded your own. He seems happy to do it on your tab.

You have waited for him to settle down, get married and have kids but at 35, he shows no signs of slowing down. He says he is having too much fun.

You have told him that we are not here to have fun. You have explained to him the many benefits of marriage and children, without success.

Your lawyer says that this is very common. Many sons have formed the view that marriage is a mug's game, and kids make your life a misery. You do not know where they got that impression.

Left to his own devices, your son would quickly spend his inheritance. Then where would you be?

NOW LET'S HEAR THE ARGUMENT FOR THE ROAST BEEF
Brennan
律師
MRS JUSTICE SMITH WAITED FOR HER HUSBAND TO DECIDE WHAT HE WANTED FOR DINNER

Your lawyer advises that an "Alcotestamentary" trust clause be inserted in your will. On your death, your son's part of the inheritance would be managed by a trustee until he sobers up, if ever. The right trustee will look after your son and give him his inheritance in very sensible small installments. The real problem is choosing the right trustee.

His siblings may be too soft. An accountant is an excellent choice and will often add little lectures in money management which I understand are quite tortuous. However, that does cost money.

The best choice by far is an ex-girlfriend, especially one who fears that she has been left on the shelf as a result of your son's dithering. Combine the ex-girlfriend with a narrow minded religious friend of the family and your money should be quite safe, especially if you provide that the trustees' decisions are to be unanimous.

The right choice of trustee has been the first step on the path of sobriety for many wayward sons.

WHAT TO TELL THE CHILDREN

I am often asked if the content of a will should be revealed to adult children. In a perfect world, my answer is absolutely not. This will allow you to change your will for petty reasons e.g. that they did not ask you to lunch, without upsetting them or appearing senile.

If the reason for changing your will is a good one, they can be informed after the will has been changed and they have lost out. The more money that they think you have, the more satisfying this can be. You can always change it back later.

But as clients get older and their fortunes greater they come under increasing pressure from their adult children to reveal "Who to?" and "How much?". Trying to reason with an adult child that their "utterly useless" sibling is more deserving is not accepted as a valid reason for the loss or reduction of their rightful inheritance. When a step mother or step child is involved, such explanations will fall on deaf ears.

PROBATE DEPT.
SWINE FLU?
NO, THEY ALWAYS LOOK LIKE THAT
律師
Brennan

If you tell each of your adult children that they shall receive their full share whether or not that is true, you may later come under pressure to produce the will. The solution is for your lawyer to produce several wills in different terms. The appropriate will can be left around the house on a visit by an adult child. A little bit like changing the photographs on display. To stop your children conferring, each will must say that everything is left to that particular child.

As a will provides that any previous will is invalid, it is just a matter of having the will that you really want to be dated later than the bogus wills and kept safely at your lawyer's office.

In these circumstances, a child that has lost out may challenge your will on the grounds of your insanity. However, most judges will accept that you were driven to distraction by your children. Not an uncommon occurrence.

WHAT ABOUT IF YOU DIE FIRST?
I DON'T THINK WE NEED TO WORRY ABOUT THAT
律師
PBrennan
THE BLACK WIDOWS MAKE THEIR WILLS

THE DAUGHTER-IN-LAW (DIL)

If you could sum up your DIL in one word would it be "gin-sodden"? Is she:

- A shopaholic and Oprah addict?
- A lazy slattern who dumps the kids on you when it suits her?
- An evil witch who deliberately restricts access to your grandchildren to make you suffer?
- An hysterical nagger of your only son?

But for your kindliness and the restraint that you have shown over the years, the family relationship would have gone to pot.

You worry that on your death if you leave your money to your son, she will blow it. What if by the time of your death they have split up and her lawyer claims the inheritance as part of the divorce settlement?

You could leave it to your grandchildren, but you know what that lot are like.

WELL, NO WE HAD NOT REALLY THOUGHT ABOUT A DIVORCE
律師
Brennan
LAWYER COCKTAIL PARTY SMALL TALK

One way is to leave your money in your will on trust to your son and grandchildren only. This is called a "testamentary trust." You can appoint your son as trustee but it may be better to appoint your brother or your lawyer to be the trustee with discretion on how much to give each year, if anything. If you are feeling cruel, appoint your accountant.

There is a lot of satisfaction in immediately telling your DIL your succession arrangements. But she may seek revenge by trying to commit you to a home at the first signs of dementia.

Therefore, it is best to leave it as a surprise. Alternatively, tell her you are just thinking about it and see if she picks up her act.

But if this all seems too hard, there is a lot to be said for telling her that you are leaving your money to your son in the usual way and then proceeding to spend it frivolously.

CONCLUSION

Despite successfully managing to trudge through this Book, many of you will still encounter avoidable will and inheritance problems in your own family.

Whether you are a modern assertive woman or a sensitive soul who can resort to old fashioned nagging for a good cause, you are now armed with sufficient information to protect your family from much upset and stress.

Even just dropping it into the conversation can ensure that you have the satisfaction of saying, "I told you so." Unlike many other things in life, the more money that you have the more miserable the "Succession Planning" process can be. Your lawyer can be a ray of sunshine in the whole process, hard to believe I know.

All the best,

Paul Brennan
Sunshine Coast, Queensland
January 2015

I SHOULD HAVE BEEN RUDER AND EVEN MORE BAD TEMPERED
律師
Brennan
A DYING JUDGE REGRETS

NEED A SPEAKER FOR YOUR CONFERENCE, ORGANISATION Or CLUB?

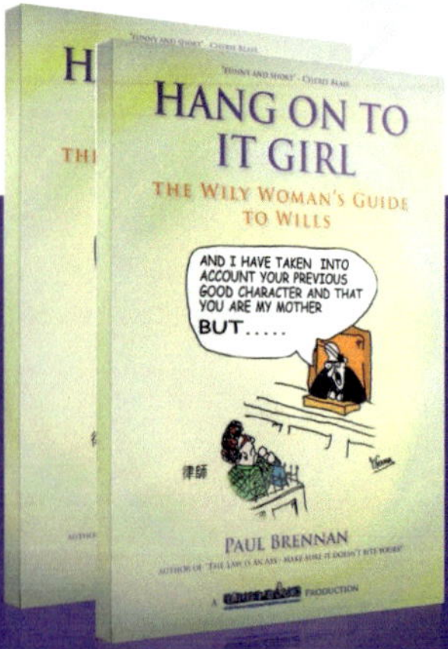

In an entertaining, humorous style Paul Brennan highlights the biggest legal traps in succession planning, traps that can cost your family your fortune to resolve - and which all too frequently can destroy families.

You will learn:

- How to avoid turning your children from best friends to sworn enemies
- How to deal with spendthrift, drunken, philandering partners or children
- How to stop your daughter in law running off with your money

"Paul turned legal mysteries into understandable entertainment."

- *Maroochy Zonta Club*

"fantastic value, fun, great listening"

THE 10 GREATEST LEGAL MISTAKES IN BUSINESS *...and how to avoid them*

AUDIO CD PLUS EBOOK

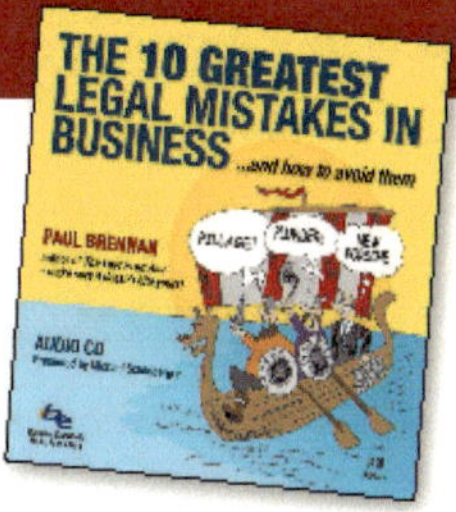

It is difficult for even the most creative business person to commit entirely new legal mistakes. They've all been done before - many, many times. Often people wait until they are desperate before they see a lawyer about a legal problem - this just seems to be human nature. But you don't need to learn the hard way. **You can avoid legal mistakes if you know what is coming.**

Paul Brennan, author of *The Law is an Ass - make sure it doesn't bite yours!* lists the top 10 legal mistakes in business - plus other legal minefields. And it couldn't be easier. You can listen to the CD and then reinforce the key messages by reading the eBook.

YOU WILL LEARN HOW TO:

- **Take the pain out of partnership disputes**
- **Avoid disaster when buying a business**
- **Benefit from "restraint of trade" clauses**
- **Negotiate leases**
- **Use trade marks to protect your business name**
- **Prevent the theft of your business secrets**
- **Survive a computer contract**
- **Mediate to settle disputes**
- **Manage litigation - the last resort!**

A fantastic way to learn the tricks and traps in the law. Paul's succinct yet humorous delivery makes a hard subject easy to understand - and the eBook is a fabulous resource to remind us about the lessons. Every business will benefit!

Michael Schildberger, Business Essentials

Paul Brennan is not only a practising business lawyer but a legal columnist with My Business Magazine and a regular commentator on Business Essentials, a monthly CD for growing small to medium sized businesses.

ORDER FORM

1 CD + eBook	Total $24.95 (plus $1.00 p&h)	5 CDs + eBooks	Total $115.00 (plus $1.00 p&h)
10 CDs + eBooks	Total $210.00 (plus $2.50 p&h)	25 CDs + eBooks	Total $500.00 (plus $6.75 p&h)
100 CDs + eBooks	Total $1750.00 (plus $6.75 p&h)	(All prices inclusive of GST in Australia)	

Yes, I would like to order _________ CDs plus eBooks

YOUR DETAILS

Name: __________ Organisation: __________

Phone: __________ Fax: __________

Address: __________

Country: (if not Australia) __________ Postcode: __________

Email: __________ Today's Date: __________

METHOD OF PAYMENT

☐ Visa ☐ Mastercard ☐ Cheque ☐ AMEX

Name on Card: __________ Signature: __________

Card Number: ☐☐☐☐ ☐☐☐☐ ☐☐☐☐ ☐☐☐☐ Expiry Date: ______ / ______

Fax, mail or telephone your order to: Business Essentials Pty Ltd, ABN 98 006 144
405 Riversdale Road, Hawthorn East Vic 3123, Australia • Tel: 61-3 9882 8333 • Freefax 1800 656 351 • Freecall 1800 039 098

CONTACT US ON

(07) 5438 8199 or

email: info@lawanddisorder.com.au

SPONSORED by

www.brennanlaw.com.au

Made in the USA
Las Vegas, NV
09 November 2026

57757225R00024